ANGER MANAGEMENT

12 Step Guide to Recognize and Control Anger, Develop Emotional Intelligence, and Self-Discipline

RAY VADEN

ANGER MANAGEMENT

12 Step Guide to Recognize and Control Anger, Develop Emotional Intelligence, and Self-Discipline

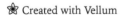 Created with Vellum

INTRODUCTION

Congratulations on downloading *Anger Management: 12 Step Guide to Recognize and Control Anger, Develop Emotional Intelligence, and Self-Discipline*, and thank you for doing so. Everyone gets angry from time to time, and we could all use some advice and reminders on how to deal with anger that flares up in our lives occasionally.

You already know that anger is not a bad emotion; it is quite useful. Not many things would have changed so far had someone not been unhappy and angry about a situation. If we were all grateful for what we have, we would never see the need to do better. Anger is only harmful and destructive when it is withheld and when it gains momentum before it finally erupts through physical violence, screaming, verbal outbursts, throwing things around, and other erratic behavior. However, we can all learn how to control anger in its infancy to keep it from wearing its ugly face and destroying our lives and our relationships.

To that end, the following chapters will teach you how to accept and understand your angry feelings. You will learn why it is necessary that you own up to what you are feeling before proceeding to deal with establishing controls. Examples of ways to control anger include pausing before you react or respond, expressing your anger calmly, and developing empathy towards the offenders so that you are able to understand their viewpoint which somehow decreases the intensity of the anger you have within you.

Besides control, you have the option of letting out the anger by redirecting your focus from the anger and onto more important things that will bring you happiness. Any pent-up anger needs to be released, ideally, in a creative manner. Instead, you ought to create room for mistakes so that you are not too hard on yourself and others around you. You will also learn how to let go of the anger and hurt by forgiving and letting go entirely in a way that takes the emotion out of the negative experiences, to allow you to move on completely, with no baggage from the past.

There are plenty of books on this subject on the market, thanks again for choosing this one! Every effort was made to ensure it is full of as much useful information as possible. Please enjoy!

❧ I ❧

ACCEPT YOUR ANGER

The advancements and developments we have seen in our society have made us a comfort-seeking lot, and when things are not done our way, we flip out easily. We want the delivery guy to be on time, we want our partners to behave as though they were us, we get upset when the professor does not award us the grade we wanted, we want our children not to speak back at us, we get upset when our favorite show does not show –there are too many reasons.

No one likes the emotional burden that anger brings. We want to spring back to good emotions as soon as possible. In our strive for comfort, we do not want to experience painful emotions, and instead, we take up different coping habits, a majority of which are harmful, like shopping too much, gambling, overeating, and alcohol and drug abuse. These habits are meant to numb our feelings.

It must not be news to you to realize that avoiding emotions does not work. Whatever technique you take up to numb yourself, however, you are only likely to make your life more difficult. You also lose out on the important lessons that the negative emotions stand to teach you in regards to the decisions you have made, the manner in which you are living your life and the changes you ought to effect to improve your life. The problem with exposing your emotions is that society is likely to label or refer to you as someone with a problem. People assume that something is wrong with you if you express anger. They say you are having 'issues.' This is partly the reason why many people like to hide their anger or want to spring back to the good times quickly without processing the negative emotions they have had.

Researchers have studied the reason for taking the time to take in and process all kinds of emotions. They believe that having a jolly mood, optimism, or being happy all the time does not guarantee the stability of your emotional health. Instead, you ought to feel all your emotions in a balanced way, to achieve a sense of wholeness, and to learn how to manage life's twists and turns. It is said that learning how to tolerate distress and discomfort is even more important than the pursuit of happiness.

Many people fear expressing anger. They see it as a sign that they have lost control of life or failed in character, as though anger would drive them to anxiety thinking that the anger would force them into a rage. We are also conditioned, right from our childhood, that it is wrong to get angry. Whenever a child throws a temper tantrum, whether big or small, he or she gets punished for it. This teaches them that anger is bad and that they should refrain from expressing it. As an adult, whenever you display your anger, people avoid you and do not want to associate with you. Because of these negative reactions, we all want to remain jolly all day, refusing to acknowledge the negative feelings when they come up.

Nevertheless, researchers point to some benefits of feeling your anger emotions. Taking in your feelings of anger enables you to view the world more optimistically seeing that people who are able to accept their feelings of anger are more likely to take risks and plunge into unfamiliar situations.

People are provoked to take action and cause a change in the world only when they become angry because of what they can see. Altruism is likely to have developed from anger because it brings together different kinds of people and generates support for a particular cause. In some situations, anger can enhance performance and be a source of leverage in negotiations. Sometimes, it even raises the level of creativity.

Rarely does anger lead to violence. Instead, anger becomes a source of encouragement and it motivates you to defend yourself when your rights are threatened. When expressed properly, it can also be a way to ask the adversary to back off.

On the contrary, when you bury feelings of anger, you not only dampen the negative ones, you also do positive emotions like joy.

WHAT IT MEANS TO ACCEPT YOUR ANGER

Most people get angry and let everyone know their thoughts. Others say silly, stupid, and regretful things that they have to acknowledge and apologize for later shamefully. Getting angry, for us, is always about finding the external culprit and letting him or her know that they caused the anger and that you are not to blame.

However, accepting anger means taking an inward look at yourself. It requires you to spend time with your negative emotions so that you understand what is going on. Begin taking note of anger from its onset in the form of annoyances and irritations. Whenever you feel these emotions rising, take a moment to determine their triggers. Seek to know precisely what is causing you to feel as you are: there is always an underlying need that has not been met.

Once you follow through your anger, you will come to find out the things that are buried deep that you should have dealt with a long time ago. These things have been the reasons for the patterns in your life, which are likely to have limited your growth. Therefore, accepting your feelings will only improve you and help you overcome traumas from your past.

THE PROCESS OF ACCEPTING YOUR FEELINGS

This process is broken down into the following smaller steps:

1. Take note of the feelings you have and don't consider ignoring them.

Although this may be painful, you need to know how to confront your feelings and examine your situation realistically.

2. Take a break to boost your emotional health

Begin to think of how you can bring down the stress and emotional turmoil you are going through. You could use this time to do the things that you find fun. Physical exercise is a critical component of this downtime. It will help you work off your feelings.

3. Speak to your family

Share the opinions you have with your family. Let them know the progress you have made in dealing with the problem and with your emotions of anger. Talking provides you with an opportunity to express what you are feeling, to vent, and to accept better, the feelings you have been having. A family is a source of both reassurance and support to help you rebuild your self-esteem.

4. Speak to other people

Talking to other people, particularly those who have been in the situation you are before will provide you with the assistance you need. You also find that you are not struggling with the issue alone; many others are doing the same.

5. Maximize the use of your time

Some habits are detrimental to your time usage such as spending a lot of time watching television or drowning yourself on the internet. Think about the number of times you felt that you should have done some things better such as spending time with your children. Do some reading, go fishing, begin projects around the house, or take up that course you always wanted to.

At first, you may lack the drive or the will to try out these things. However, once your feelings have died down, take the opportunity, and put your time to good use. Working on the activities you do will bring you more satisfaction in life or bring you a new talent that will make you more productive.

EVALUATE THE SITUATION

If the situation you are in looks like it will be the same for a while, shift your focus and start thinking of alternatives. You may require help analyzing your skills to see what you are good at or to establish the need for additional training to help you pursue your desired goal, job, or career.

SEEK PROFESSIONAL HELP

The feelings brought by a loss of any kind are very strong and it may prove difficult for you to deal with them by yourself. However, discussing the issue with a professional will ease the process of working through your feelings, making recovery quicker.

UNDERSTAND YOUR ANGER

ANGER IS A NATURAL RESPONSE TRIGGERED BY THE FIGHT-
or-flight body physiology. Your body produces this emotional response
against any perceived threats. While fear is the flight response, anger
is the emotional energy that drives you to want to fight back. Surpris-
ingly, your mind will create fear and anger responses even when the
threat is not apparent when you imagine it.

IMAGINED V. REAL ANGER

Distinguishing between an imagined and a real threat can be difficult
because, on many occasions, they happen at the same time. For example, suppose you are walking on the curb headed home and a rider on
skates is swerving in your direction unable to control his speed. In a
case like this, you will produce both a fight and a flight reaction driven
by a combination of fear of the skater hitting you and the need to
protect you and him from falling. The reality of the situation and the
emotions pass very quickly, and so will your emotions.

Your mind, however, will not let you go. You will be left imagining the worst case scenarios. You start thinking about how you might have stretched a tendon while you were leaping out of his way. You begin to recall similar cases you heard about or videos you watched on the internet showing a similar situation and the dire consequences that followed. As you do this, you add more emotion to the situation and the response you give will be based on the imaginations that have been going through your mind.

You must be aware of the processes taking place in your mind, however. If you are unaware of the influence your imagination has and how it is leading you to project these scenarios in your head, you are likely to blame others for how you feel. Unfortunately, when anger is directed towards a false cause, it becomes a tool for destroying your life and your relationships rather than a tool that you use to protect yourself.

UNDERSTANDING YOUR ANGER

The truth is that anger is a natural response to have it just depends on how you perceive your emotions and different scenarios in the mind. It is okay to become angry, even if the situations are imagined because this is an indication that your body's emotional response system is working correctly. The issue remains to be the beliefs, thoughts, and scenarios that bring about the anger because most often, they are irrational.

Other problems come about when you are unable to refrain from anger outbursts. Reactions like these and their consequences often distract a person from the actual underlying problem. They make us believe that anger is the problem since it is what will take our attention first. However, your emotions and reactions are only an outward reaction indicating what has been going through the mind, whether real or imagined.

The way to overcome anger is to change the way your mind reacts or imagines stories. It is by controlling the extent to which these things influence your emotional wellness. For example, if the imagination of pain causes you to be frustrated and angry, the best way to eliminate the anger is to pull your thinking away from the painful memories. You also need to change or remove your assumptions, core beliefs, and mind interpretations.

MISPLACED ANGER

One of the most important things to note about anger is that it is motivated by the desire not to experience guilt. Blaming other people for how you feel creates a thrill, an excitement, and satisfaction because you do not have to take responsibility for how you are acting or the consequences of it.

We have agreed by now that anger is a primary emotion that comes when a person feels powerless, rejected, accused, unimportant, guilty, devalued, untrustworthy, unlovable, disregarded, and many other similar sentiments. These feelings bring considerable amounts of pain, which makes it understandable that people want to distance themselves from it. Therefore, the primary role for anyone who is not willing to face, accept, and understand his anger will be to create a cover-up to avoid vulnerability. The cover-up becomes an ideal vehicle for escaping the shame, upset, or anxiety a person feels, possibly because he has not developed the emotional resources he needs to cope with the issue at hand successfully.

Looking at an example, let's assume your partner has said something, intentionally or otherwise, that caused you to feel demeaned. Rather than becoming assertive and expressing your dissatisfaction with the statement your partner has made, which could reveal your vulnerability, you react, instead, by looking for something to use to get back at him or her. When you do this, you are, in effect, launching the tit for tat war. What happens is that as you engage in their retaliatory pursuits, your negative emotions will fade away. Worked? Well, yeah, but not quite. This only reinforces the childlike behavior of blaming each other endlessly, instead of each partner taking responsibility.

But looking at this example again, from your partner's perspective, what will happen to his or her temper? Your partner becomes the new bearer for the emotional baggage you have just successfully shed. Whatever feelings you had, you have transferred them to the partner. After this happens, your partner instinctively develops both hurt and fear. The fear comes about because he is now turned into an object of anger, and he subconsciously now thinks that you intend to harm him. Therefore, if you observe that taking out your frustrations on other people, it is not because they want to give you space to process your emotions, it is because they are instinctively led to keep a distance from anything that could harm them, psychologically, physically, and in any other way.

Some people are not as calm and will respond to your attack with an equal and opposite defensive attack. This is called counter-retaliation. The partner starts to blame you too, and this could result in a serious conflict, verbal or otherwise.

To change this uncomfortable cycle, you need to get a hold of what drives you into anger. You also need to study its effects. Surely, you cannot go about life retaliating towards every jab thrown at you. Instead, learn how to hold on to your most rational self and peacefully process whatever is happening.

❧ 3 ☙

PAUSE BEFORE YOU REACT

A LARGE PROPORTION OF YOUR LIFE HAS BEEN DETERMINED by the reactions you gave to things or people around you. Majority of these reactions are not the best courses of action, and because of this, we end up making ourselves or/and others unhappy. Some even make the situation worse.

We say the first thing that land in our mouths first without giving it a thought. We become defensive and are quick to talk back, which worsens the situation. In other areas of life, we are quick to put food in our mouths before thinking about how the foods would affect the body system. We make purchasing decisions in a split second, without even caring whether our finances can support the purchases. All these common scenarios indicate clearly how often we put action before thought, especially when driven by anger.

The reaction you present is driven by a gut emotion that has resulted from insecurities and fear. This is not often the most rational way to behave. The opposite of reacting is responding, and it involves taking in the situation and making a decision on the best course of action based on reason, cooperation, and compassion.

LEARN HOW TO RESPOND

It is often said that if you speak from your anger, you will make the speech you will regret forever. The seriousness of this statement is brought by the fact that once you utter some words, you can never take them back. Although sitting down with your sadness, frustration, disappointment, grief, and anger is quite uncomfortable, you will feel so much worse once you have poured out your vile on another's face. To do this, you need to learn how to pause between anger and reaction.

This internal pause is developed by becoming mindful and living more presently. It slows down the natural reaction because when you are mindful, you focus on living in the moment and this produces so much inner peace and tranquility such that when someone comes at you with an erratic rant, you will not fly off the handle either, you will be more accepting of people and their mistakes.

When you pause, you take your time to assimilate the information or the deed that has been done before you give a response to it. A voice inside your head tells you what you would typically have voiced out, but if you give yourself a few seconds, you will realize that the nasty statement you would have made was uncalled for and wouldn't make a difference anyway.

I hate to apologize. I hate having to lower myself to the ground asking for forgiveness. It feels as though I am worshipping the other person by swallowing my pride and begging them to forgive me. This attitude grew in me after messing up too many times. Whenever my anger flared out, I would spit any venom that came into my mouth, trying to make the other party feel as downgraded and looked-down-upon as I had been made to feel. I am a naturally calm and quiet person, and if someone hurt me, the natural way to fight back would be through words, even though they were said softly.

My conscience would not let me go after that. After lashing out, what would follow is an endless battle inside me, which would end with me crawling back to the person who offended me with my tail between my legs to say sorry. I grew to hate this so much until I devised a new strategy. I decided to put a pause between anger and reaction.

Today, whenever someone does something to hurt me and I want to lash out, I remember that I will have to go through the tedious process of asking for forgiveness and I stop in my tracks. I also take in the statements that have been said or the deed that has been done and considers what would happen. In those few seconds, I realize that I do not have to retaliate and that it is my opportunity to take the high road. Sometimes, you have to hate something bad enough to want to change how you behave or do things.

Here are a few steps you can take to initiate the internal pause

1. Take note of the triggers

Realize the sensations that build up in you to indicate that you are becoming irritated and angry. It could be an increase in body heat, your stomach knotting, pulsating in the head, and a tight chest. Once you recognize these as signs that your anger has been triggered, you need to activate your internal pause immediately.

When involved in an argument and you realize that your temper and ego are flaring, simple awareness and recognition of what is happening will send it back to where it came from.

2. Pause: This step requires you to press pause in your mind as you do it on your TV using the remote.

3. Breathe deeply: A significant amount of oxygen in your brain is useful for helping you gather your thoughts and makes you mindful of the moment.

4. Look around: When interacting with people, you need to hold off your thoughts and opinions and listen. It is not mandatory for you to give an immediate response to counter what you disagree with. Just take note of the ideas that are floating around in your mind and do not get attached to any of them. For example, if you are set on reducing your spending, take your mind back to a goal you set or a mantra you created regarding a situation like this one. Think, also, of the best possible results. How would you hope that the situation will turn out? Again, allow yourself to look keenly into all the thoughts that are passing through your mind.

5. Now 'Play': Now that you have examined all the good and bad ideas that your mind has run concerning this situation, it is now time to act. You need to do this mindfully. Think about what the most compassionate, respectful, and intelligent response could be. What could you possibly say to calm everyone down and resolve the situation in a better way?

You may not be very good at this process at first, but practicing will make you perfect at it. You will get better at pausing; don't worry if there is a miss or two. If you end up replying fast, take note of the emotion or thought that caused you to do so, and keep watch in the future to ensure that you are able to pause thoughts like that.

You must be thinking that this process looks too easy and good on paper, but that it would not work in real life. In the heat of the moment, no one would be able to grow through that long process. However, this is not the case. This process has been tested and proven to be an ideal solution for people with reaction problems, which is practically the majority of the people.

Yes, the process may seem a bit too long, but if you have struggled with erratic responses, the process will help you to remember the importance of waiting before you respond. It makes a whole lot of difference because it grants you the chance to rewind, decide on a profitable course of action, and then continue your interaction in a way that makes you feel good about yourself and makes you a role model for persons with a hot temper over those that have difficulty controlling their responses.

🐾 4 🐾
EXPRESS YOUR ANGER CALMLY

MANY OF US HAVE TROUBLE MAINTAINING THEIR COOL AND respect when dealing with some volatile situations, even when you intended to. You may have begun by pausing to think of your reply, but you are now unable to maintain your cool, especially if the other side is being disrespectful, lying, or starting to behave in angry ways. However, this entire process is not intended to make you a walkover such that other people can dump their frustrations on you and you only respond with happy, inspirational quotes: you are also allowed to express your negative feelings of anger, frustration, disappointment, and others, but just do it calmly.

Let's look at an example. Last year, my friend Jane found a suspicious text on her husband's cellphone and she suspected that he was having an affair. When she confronted him later in the day, the man reluctantly confessed to having sex with an old friend he had recently reconnected with. Jane was overcome with anger. She asked her husband to leave the house, but the man knelt, began to cry, and apologize, assuring her that he loved only her, not the other woman. Jane was overcome with emotion, and she allowed him to stay.

In the days that followed, anger was boiling inside of her. She felt that she couldn't express it, seeing that she had accepted his apology. So, whenever the negative feelings flared up, she bottled them and continued to treat him as though everything was okay between them. Part of her wanted to out her feelings of frustration and disappoint-ment while the other felt that anger was unnecessary. She wanted to behave well, to prove to herself and the man that she was emotionally superior. However, in a couple of weeks, she became seriously sick, depressed, and she was experiencing mental and emotional fatigue.

Many of us have been like Jane because we have learned that expressing anger erratically, the only way we knew how to, is uncool. But, is it fair to keep these emotions bottled inside? We fear that if we express anger in our way, we will hurt those around us. If we keep it in, we beat ourselves. Science shows that when you get angry, the body secretes stress hormones, and if they are just circulating in the body, they will increase your propensity to cardiovascular disease and infections. So, what is the solution?

The most appropriate beneficial way to deal with anger is to express it in a healthy way so that you can turn this pent-up destructive energy into constructive action. Neuroscientists have confirmed that when-ever we put the negative feelings we have into words, the activity of the amygdala (the emotions and decision-making part of the brain), decreases and this process enhances our physical and mental health. Evidence has also shown that people who openly express their emotions and feelings are naturally healthier than those who suppress them.

How should you go about expressing your anger in a calm way that will not hurt you or other people? Here are some positive, construc-tive ways that you can use to do it.

PUT WORDS TO YOUR ANGER USING THE GESTALT TECHNIQUE

The gestalt technique involves putting a chair across from where you are sitting, imagining that the person who made you angry is seated on that seat and telling the imaginary person everything that you have bottled up. Scream at the chair. Talk to it.

Another way to do it is to set a few plump pillows on your sofa. Pretend that they are the person that has made you angry. It is best to do this one when home alone. Now, hit those pillows, scream at them, picturing the person you are unhappy with.

In only a few minutes of doing these activities, your bottled up emotions will vent and you will relax.

- **Speak to the person you are angry with**

Sometimes, people do not realize the hurt and harm that they are causing you, or they could be doing it intentionally. However, whichever the case, they need to be called out on it. You need to sit down with the person and calmly air out your frustration about what the person did. When doing this, watch out for blaming and name calling. Before you do this, you may need to release your anger through two or three of the other methods described.

- **Write a letter**

This is a beneficial method. I have personally used it more than a dozen times. It involves getting all your angry feelings out onto the paper by writing exactly how you feel. Once the emotions are on the paper, they no longer have the freedom to roll around your body causing you physical and psychological harm.

Writing is also of benefit because once ideas start flowing one after the other, you will gain clarity which is another advantage. You are also able to get into it which is good for people who are unable to express themselves well through speech.

- **Vent to a friend**

Nothing beats a supportive friend when you are angry and ranting about something. It is therapeutic to talk to someone who will see things from your perspective, but in the end, give you an objective solution to your problem. Warn your friend that you are going to pour out all your frustrations, and when you get that opportunity, ensure that you exaggerate to get all the emotion out.

However, don't let the venting become a habit. If you are continually venting, particularly about the same issues, it ceases to be therapeutic and turns into recontamination. It will no longer be right for you.

- **Scream into a pillow**

THIS METHOD IS RELATIVELY COMMON. FROM EXPERIENCE, however, I have learned that you may want to announce the scream before you do it. You are likely to scare bloody Mary out of those around you. Now, go ahead and do it.

- **Sing your anger out**

LISTEN AND SING ALONG TO MUSIC THAT CARRIES THE emotions away. If you are going through a breakup, for example, you could listen to *"Since You Been Gone"* by Kelly Clarkson or *Don't Come*

Back by Tarrus Riley. You could also involve your creative faculties and come up with your own lyrics to express exactly how you feel. Once you do this, use your voice along with any musical instrument you play to sing away your feelings.

- **Paint or draw something**

IN MANY ART CLASSES, STUDENTS ARE ASKED TO PAINT OR draw what they feel. This is a technique used to channel the inner person so that you may bring out your innermost feelings. Go ahead and do it. Draw or paint whatever comes to mind, and as you take out that pent up energy, you will realize that the feelings of anger will fade away.

- **Dance your emotions out**

DANCE UNTIL YOU FEEL FREE ON THE INSIDE. YOU COULD try doing this at your home or at a dance studio, wherever you would be comfortable with.

꙳ 5 ꙳

PRACTICE EMPATHY

Developing empathy is a great way to keep you from developing anger. When I talk of empathy, I mean being simultaneously walking in the footsteps of your aggressor, thinking about how difficult it must be for him or her, picturing the aggressor's anguish, pain, and the ordeal he or she must have gone through. The more accurately you are able to reflect the intensity and tone of emotion, the more the other person will feel understood. Therefore, to give an appropriate response, you must listen to the person using both your heart and your head.

The words that you use will show that you understand. Below are some phrases you can include in your conversation to show empathy:

"How may I help?"

"I feel that you are hurting because…"

"I cannot imagine how it must feel to …"

SOME OF THE WORDS YOU CAN USE TO INDICATE HOW THE individual is feeling include frustrated, riled, angry, infuriated, betrayed, trapped, upset, furious, exasperated, and outraged.

THE MORE PRECISE YOUR IDENTIFICATION AND reflection of the emotions the person is feeling the better their release of the negative energy, which means that the person will not project his or her anger at you. When a person feels heard, he feels supported, he relaxes, and he begins the healing journey to regain his poise.

THE IMPORTANCE OF EMPATHY

Neuroscientists have found that a person is wired to take in empathy through the many mirror neurons located in the brain. These neurons reflect the actions we observe in other people, causing us to simulate these same actions in our brains. Whenever you see someone in pain, you are likely to feel that pain, to a similar extent as that person, and when you observe a happy person, you are likely to become happy to the same degree. The mirroring of these neurons is the basis for empathy because it creates a wave that connects our emotions to those people around us.

SOME PEOPLE ARE EMPATHETIC BY NATURE, WHILE OTHERS are not. The good thing is that empathy can be learned. Here are the five steps to getting over anger using empathy: (as you go through the stages below, picture yourself interacting with an angry person who is lashing out at you).

- **Stop, take a breather and set an agenda**

You NEED TO PAUSE AND TAKE A FEW DEEP BREATHS SO that you are able to channel all your attention to the present moment. When you do this, you will also get the opportunity to use your imagination to come up with an intention or a goal for how you would want the situation to play in the end. At a minimum, the intention should be to listen, understand, and connect with the other party throughout your interaction. Let your agenda be that when the meeting ends, you will feel good about the composure you maintained and the fact that you took control of the situation with the ability to listen carefully and respond to the other party empathetically.

- **Observe the words you say to yourself**

THE WORDS YOU SPEAK TO YOURSELF HAVE IMMENSE POWER and they are of different kinds. Some are blaming thoughts. Some are judging thoughts, while others are discouraging thoughts among others. For example, after talking, you could find yourself saying, "How silly is he/she?" "What a jerk!" Take note of thoughts like those and be careful not to engage that line of thinking. Instead, refocus on to your initial agenda, which was to listen and connect with the person empathetically while retaining a calm presence. Remind yourself that what the other party said has more to do with him or her than with you. Therefore, whatever was said, choose to keep a distance and not take any of it personally.

- **Be in communication with your needs and feelings**

WHEN YOU ARE ABLE TO ESTABLISH A CONNECTION WITH your feelings and needs, you make the entire process real rather than just telling a person that you understand his or her perspective. Ask yourself what are you feeling exactly? From which part of your body are the feelings originating? What do you want to get out of a situation like this? Remember that if your inner self starts to judge, blame, and put negative labels on the other person, your anger will likely be triggered too.

INSTEAD, STRUCTURE YOUR THOUGHTS TO RESEMBLE THE following statement: When my friend said that I am always late, I felt terrible because I only get late trying to get her favorite coffee at the store near my house, and there is always a long queue.

NOTICE THE STRUCTURE: WHEN ___ (OBSERVATION), I feel_____ (feeling) because _____ (need).

- **Relate to other people's feelings and needs**

ONCE YOU HAVE CONNECTED WITH YOUR OWN NEEDS AND feelings, you now have to connect with what the other needs and feels. Try to think of what they would need to feel safe. It is likely that the person could be feeling frustrated because he or she was not taken seriously when trying to deliver a point the person considered important. Hence, the person interpreted that you are not keen on his or her feelings.

. . .

ALTERNATIVELY, INSTEAD OF RELYING ON ASSUMPTIONS and basing your thoughts on unconfirmed possibilities, you should go ahead to seek clarification from the other party to know precisely what could have led him or her to feel as he or she does. You will not know the problem for sure until you are able to verbalize your thoughts and seek clarification.

- Make your assumptions heard

SEE HOW YOU UNDERSTAND AND INTERPRET THE FEELINGS and emotional needs that the other person displayed. If you think someone is going through something, go ahead and ask, as the previous point suggests.

FOR EXAMPLE, ASK, "ARE YOU ANGRY WITH ME BECAUSE YOU wanted me to go get you the items from the store and I couldn't read into the urgency of your request?"

- Beware Of the Limits

SOME PEOPLE, HOWEVER, ARE SO EMPATHETIC THAT THEY forget about their own suffering and pain. Extreme empathy causes you to accommodate and understand disrespect and inappropriate behavior because you feel compelled to forgive and forget the disrespect to the point where you act as if nothing happened.

IT IS EASY TO FORGET YOURSELF WHEN YOU ARE FOCUSING

too much on how another person is feeling. Because you are suffering too much, you relate to the individual's pain and somehow become absorbed into their world. This can go to extremes where you begin to fantasize and create stories that would somehow excuse the person's behavior. You start to think about the possible bad upbringing the person had, how the individual must have been left to his own devices, you begin to imagine the insecurity issues the person could have or the undiagnosed psychological issues that the person might have. Extreme empathy gets you on a frantic search looking for reasons to excuse negative behavior at your expense.

EMPATHY EITHER EMPOWERS YOU EMOTIONALLY OR NUMBS you. It is admirable to be able to connect with other people's pain, emotions, pasts, and experiences, but there is a limit to it. As much as you are able to communicate with other people's pains, you need to stop for a minute and connect to yours too. You matter, you are of value, and you are responsible for nurturing your beautiful self, sometimes, even before you take care of other people.

IN SUMMARY, DEVELOPING EMPATHY IS THE DECISION YOU make on whether to let your defense mechanisms take over or whether to shift your emotions and thoughts in your body and mind so that you and the agitated person who is around can calm down. It is not easy in any way, but when you realize the dynamics of empathy, you will want to adapt it as a useful tool to be used for the rest of your life.

⚜ 6 ⚜

REDIRECT YOUR FOCUS

ANGER IS ONE OF THE STRONGEST EMOTIONS A PERSON can feel because it provides them with push, power, drive, and motivation. However, research shows that 1 in every 5 Americans has an anger management problem, that 65% of the office employees have experienced office rage, and that 45% have lost their temper at work.

At worst, anger can be quite frustrating and it can be an obstacle to performance and success. At best, anger is the force that drives us to success, and ultimately, to happiness. The trick lies in the ability to convert the negative energy into a positive emotion that will inspire you to experience positive results or in redirecting your focus entirely to avoid its path completely. Here's how to do it:

CHECK YOURSELF

When under the leadership and control of a dominant negative emotion, it can be difficult to make smart decisions. Instead of having to talk yourself down from a cliff, how about not climbing the cliff in the first place? Take note of your anger triggers and the signs that will indicate to you that you are on the verge of getting angry. When you see these things coming up, walk away from that situation, and get yourself to relax and calm down to keep the irritation from escalating.

STOP DWELLING ON WHAT HAS HAPPENED

Some people have no problem rehashing an incident that happened and caused them to be angry. This is unproductive especially when the issue has already been resolved and the outcome of the situation already determined without a chance of revocation. You need to let go of what happened, and instead, focus on the things you appreciate about the case or the person that angered you. The change in focus is significant because it helps to take out the negative emotions and helps you to maintain your peace.

CHANGE YOUR COGNITION

Cognition refers to how you think. When you are angry, it is easy to imagine that things are even worse than they appear. You become overly dramatic and tend to exaggerate everything. However, you can turn back to rationality by replacing your negative thoughts to positive ones using a technique called cognitive restructuring. Instead of thinking, "my life is ruined, I have lost everything, everybody hates me, I am no good," tell yourself, "I am sad, but this is only a setback. It is understandable that I feel upset about it. It does not indicate the end of my world or my life. Getting angry will not fix my situation."

Avoid using words like 'always' and 'never' when you are upset and talking about yourself or about someone else. You cannot tell someone, "You always forget important things," or mutter, "This terrible washer never works." These statements are most likely false and are only meant to justify your anger, but they do not resolve the problem that you have. They also effectively alienate people you could otherwise be working with to come up with a solution.

Always keep in mind the fact that anger does not resolve anything and that reacting to it will not make you feel better either. You are even likely to feel worse.

Seek to lean towards logic always, rather than anger. Even when you are truly justified to be angry, you can easily switch and become irrational. Instead, even when you are mad, rely on cold facts to remind yourself that you are not just a victim and that there is more to life than what you are experiencing. The challenges you are facing are common to man, and that they are only the rough spots of daily living. Remind yourself of these facts whenever your anger flares up so that you achieve some objectivity in your perspective.

Another critical thing to help you avoid anger is to get rid of your sense of entitlement. You are likely to get angry when you demand things and they are not availed to you. For example, you may become angry because your secretary forgot to sort out your mail, possibly because she was too busy handling other tasks related to your office or just because she forgot. Getting angry because of this is irrational because if you were, to be honest, you also forget things sometimes or you may have too many responsibilities at a time and choose to prioritize the important ones. If you become angry, your secretary will start to think that her contribution does not matter much and that you do not trust his or her judgment to prioritize and make decisions in the office. Her motivation to work will reduce significantly and so could her productivity. Instead of getting angry and affecting the environment around you, voice your concern with kindness, and she will go out of her way next time to ensure that your mail is sorted.

Adopt better skills for communication. When people get angry, they are likely to mutter the meanest things that come to their minds, however unkind. Before you react, however, take a minute to stop and breathe. Give careful thought to what you intend to say, and if you feel the need to step aside from an angry conversation to calm down, do so, and then get back to the conversation.

RELAX

Simple breathing and relaxation techniques can effectively soothe angry feelings. Practice doing them in a normal situation and it will be easier to apply them in the heat of the moment. Some of these techniques include:

Attentive breathing: When you are angry, you tend to have shallow quick breaths. Therefore, to counter this, practice deep controlled slow breathing, ensuring that they rise from your belly rather than your chest.

Relax your muscles progressively: Progressive muscle relaxation involves tensing and then relaxing your muscle group one at a time. For example, if you begin working on your head muscles, proceed to your neck muscles, going downward up until you reach the muscles in your toes.

TAKE UP IMAGERY

Visualize what a relaxation experience would look like from your imagination. In the heat of an argument, visualize what the ideal situation would be, what it would look like without this conflict, and work towards achieving that.

BECOME ACTIVE

Physical exercise done in the regular is a perfect decompression tool. It burns off the excess energy, releases the extra tension, and it lowers stress levels. When your body is all relaxed and all energy resources are being used appropriately, you are less likely to have anger outbursts.

TAKE NOTE OF AND AVOID YOUR TRIGGERS

Think about the things that cause you to lose it. If you know that driving during the rush-hour gets you angry, take the train or the bus, or at least plan to make your trip at a different time of the day. If you often go to bed arguing with your spouse, avoid bringing up contentious issues in the evening. If seeing your child's messy room gets you angry, shut the door, and you won't have to see the mess.

7

CHANNEL YOUR ANGER
CREATIVELY

WHEN YOU ARE ANGRY, YOU EITHER EXPRESS OR REPRESS your feelings. A repression is a form of denial of reality because it involves shoving down the powerful negative emotions by pretending that they do not exist. When you repress anything, it goes beneath and becomes a poisonous autocrat that lurks in the shadows, awaiting an opportune moment to break free.

Anger, when repressed, becomes explosive and uncontrollable. It becomes unpredictable and a force like no other. Many times, the inner feelings of restlessness become a volcano of emotions that are repressed. Once the pressure is released, the anger comes out in a rage and the person dumps all the bile on another person without any form of control. Self-expression of this kind is quite dangerous because it causes the end or death of many significant relationships and can be detrimental to the wellbeing and health of the people involved.

Accepting and acknowledging the fact that you are angry goes a long way towards defusing the energy and the power behind it. It involves willfully facing your subconscious mind and with compassion and empathy, meeting your emotional self in your darkest expression takes out the string out of the anger. Accepting anger also means that you acknowledge its intensity and are aware that it is only a messenger of an underlying bigger issue. What's more, the simple act of acceptance opens the doorway to creativity, vitality, and wisdom.

Once you give yourself the permission and the opportunity to express your anger in a masterful way, you unlock your inner power. You take control of the situation yourself, you come alive, and you begin to express yourself creatively and passionately. In this case, we can define anger as some hidden potential that flows through you guiding you towards unleashing your potential and towards taking the path that you should have taken all along.

Steve Jobs defined creativity as the ability to create connections. According to him, a person is creative when he or she can make connections between the experiences he or she has had to come up with new things. The reason the person will be able to make that connection is that he or she can think about experiences and deduce more substance from them better than other people can. In other words, creativity is born out of connecting your experiences with the circumstances in your present to generate new ideas that will become the solutions for the future.

Being angry makes you irrational and unpredictable. You start to imagine scenarios and events that did not even occur. You think about what would happen if the situation were to play in various ways. You begin to think of how you would react and behave in each situation. This sounds like potentially fertile ground to birth creativity. Your mind and emotions run beyond their usual thresholds, beyond the things that we consider possible.

Here's what to do to unlock your creativity when you are angry:

1. *Identify an activity that could take your mind and concentration away from the things that cause you to be angry but lets you release those emotions.* Exercise is a good example, but you have the liberty to choose from among

valuable things that distract your mind, so long as they involve physical movement. It could be an interactive video game or a brisk walk in the park. Writing is also an ideal activity.

2. *Accept and embrace the negative emotions and use them to push yourself harder.* Do this for the next 10-20 minutes. During this time, avoid any positive thoughts, just let the negativity drive you to punch harder, run harder, or write better. Whatever you do, keep going. You will find that it is easier to 'get into the zone' driven by the negative emotions as opposed to the positive ones. Once the endorphins start running through your system, you will gradually begin to think clearer and feel better.

3. *Now that the negative pent up energy is used up, begin to think about the changes you want to effect in your life and the solutions you will be seeking.* During this time, your creativity starts to rise even higher. Allow your brain to do this process all by itself, do not be caught forcing anything. However, as you are doing your chosen physical activity, focus on the hindrances, the ambitions you have, and the obstacles you are facing. Think about these things in regards to the new personal boundaries you want to implement, a new project you want to initiate, changes you want to see a trip you plan on taking, a business idea you want to implement, or a career move you intend to make.

Be careful not to stretch yourself so much mentally while doing the same physically. Only allow ideas to flow freely as your mind clears. If nothing comes yet, do not despair, don't be stressed. The most important thing for you is that you get some experience connecting and synthesizing experiences over time so that when next something angers you, you will have the tools to work through it creatively.

The great people of our society like Nelson Mandela, Martin Luther King, Gandhi, and others like them simply tapped into their inner anger and used the energy they derived from it to bring transformation in their courses. They mastered anger and used it as an ally to guide them towards unleashing incredible creativity that led to the great mobilization of people and the fight towards making an incredible mark in society.

Just because you know that anger is beneficial does not mean that you should go around seeking for reasons to be angry. It doesn't mean that anger is useful in all situations and circumstances. There are situations in which expressing your anger will even lower the respect that others accord to you in society. The first thing you need to do as you learn about anger is to differentiate between reasonable and unreasonable anger.

Take note of the events and circumstances that you can change and those that you cannot. If you are walking in the park and a strong wind blows your hat off so that it falls into fountain water, there is nothing you can do about that, which means it will do you no good to express your negative emotions. However, if someone comes and snatches your hat, you have control over the situation: you can ask for your hat back or chase the person down if you can.

Whatever you do, ensure that your anger expression is justifiable.

❧ 8 ❧

RELEASE ANGER WITH EXERCISE

PHYSICAL EXERCISE IS RATED AMONG THE MOST EFFECTIVE methods of taking down stress and anger. When exercising, you get the opportunity to let go of your emotions, especially when you feel the pressure building up fast and about to explode. Exercise lowers the stress levels, too, by causing the body to produce endorphins, the feel-good hormones that boost your mood. Exercising also gives you an opportunity to think about what prompted you to be angry in the first place and what you would want to do about it.

Here are some exercises you can engage in to release the anger:

Boxing

Boxing is one of the best ways to let out your aggression and rage while benefitting from the burning of calories. It can also be a great way to learn how to defend yourself. One of the famous gymnasts recommends hitting the heavy bag for 30- to 60-seconds intervals of all-effort before you take a 30-to 90-seconds rest. Do this repeatedly 6 to 10 times in a session. Be careful to keep your wrists straight when punching.

Medicine Ball Slams

Another therapeutic way to get rid of aggression is to slam stuff. Don't go throwing and breaking things in your house; you will have to pay for them later. Instead, do the work using a medicine ball. Here's how to do it.

Lift the medicine ball, and with a straight back and a tight core, press the ball above your head and driving strength from your core, slam the ball to the ground. The ball will bounce right back. Use this momentum to repeat the exercise without having to bend over.

Do 10- 20 slams per set, factoring in the weight of the ball. Complete 4 set.

You are cautioned that if the medicine ball you are using is made of rubber, be careful so that you do not get smacked in the face. Instead, lean over and pick it up.

Deadlifting

Deadlifting is simply lifting some weight and putting it back to the ground. Very simple. You will feel very capable once you can raise a weight and not get overwhelmed by it.

To do it, ensure that your back is straight and that your core is tight. Sit back on your heels and drive through them, pulling the bar right up to your standing position. Squeeze your glute muscles at the top, and then lower the weight just as you lifted it. To ensure that you are engaging the right muscles, ensure that the bar grazes your legs the entire time.

When working with a weight that challenges you, do 3 or 4 sets each made up of 6 to 8 reps. Your anger will go away and your muscles will become stronger.

Hill Sprints

No matter what drove you to anger, once you go up a hill running in a sprint at maximum speed, sometimes, you will have no choice but to relax at the end of it.

How to do it, pick a hill and mark a finish line for the distance that would take you 20 to 30 seconds to run at maximum speed. Run this distance the fastest you can up, walk back down as you catch your breath, and then run up the hill again. Your rests should take only between 60 and 90 seconds and you should be back in the ascent immediately that time is spent.

For maximum effect, do the exercise 6 to 10 times. If you do not live up a hill, choose to do it in a flight of stairs or set your treadmill to a steep incline. Now, go ahead and try it.

Sledgehammer Twists

This exercise is best performed using an old tractor tire lying on its side if you can find one. This exercise is a great way to build muscle strength, to burn calories, and of course, to let out the anger. Most people swear by it, saying it beats exercising on the treadmill tremendously.

If you cannot get your hands on the old tire, use a woodchopper. It uses the same motion, only that you do the exercise with a medicine ball and not a tractor tire.

To do this exercise effectively using a sledgehammer, swing it as you would a baseball bat, and you will feel the effects of the swing and a release of the built-in emotions.

Yoga

Yoga is an exercise that works to purify and enhance the wellness of the mind, the soul, and the body. It is a spiritual approach to anger that, depending on its intensity, can be quite an intense workout by stretching the body, focusing on your breathing, and increasing your flexibility. In the course of doing all that, the anger you have built in will just melt away. One particular pose, the warrior pose, is a powerful stance that could cause you to release all the sadness and anger within. It focuses on instilling courage and balance which you could particularly use now.

Aerobics

Aerobics are some of the most useful high-energy workouts. They get your heart pumping, reduce blood pressure, and ease your anxiety. You could try skipping rope, cycling, the treadmill or jogging at the park.

Walking Briskly

WHENEVER I FEEL LIKE I NEED TO CLEAR MY MIND, I GO for a walk. The primary reason I choose to walk is that I do not like to jog or run; aerobics are not my thing. Instead, I take a 30-minutes walk, which can be turned to an hour's walk, sometimes. Walking significantly lowers the level of your stress hormones, breaks down calories, and improves on your agility.

WALKING IS ALSO ONE OF THE BEST ACTIVITIES TO DO IF you need to spend some time alone for self-reflection. Because when you are alone with your thoughts, you are able to connect with yourself. You do not have to think about the problem you are dealing with during your walk, focus on you only, and when the internal systems are working well, you will make a sound decision about the issues once you get back.

BEGIN BY TAKING A 20-MINUTES WALK, AT LEAST THRICE A week, and increase this time gradually.

🎋 9 🎋

GIVE YOURSELF A BREAK

OUR SOCIETY ENCOURAGES US TO BE ON THE GO ALL THE time. Faster, higher, and better are used too often to indicate to us the pace of life we should maintain. If you are offended, it is best to get over your anger sooner. You are advised to become better at withstanding sad things like discouragement and heartbreak so that you can move forward faster. However, in our haste, we forget to give ourselves room to breathe and be.

MANY OF US WILL FEEL THE PRESSURE MOUNTING, BUT WE cannot stand to take a moment to slow down or rest because then, we won't be branded as successful, we won't be liked, our value will go down, and if you do not overcome your hurt fast enough, people will not talk about what an amazing heart you got. It would seem like the more you bear, the more relevant you become. However, what happened to resting for a while? How about if you would just take some time to be by yourself and process your emotions slowly?

. . .

FOR YOU TO GIVE YOURSELF THE BREAK YOU DESPERATELY need, you need to have compassion on yourself. Having compassion means that you are aware of the suffering you are going through. You are aware of who you are and you are responding to the pain you are going through with kindness, love, and gentleness.

PSYCHOLOGISTS HAVE DISCOVERED SELF-COMPASSION TO be a performance enhancement tool in different settings, from the corporate field to athletics. It even has aging benefits. People with self-compassion also tend to have higher esteem although the sense of self-importance it brings is innate and is not dependent on a comparison between yourself and other people. People are now beginning to take care of themselves and their wellbeing genuinely, and eventually, they recover from their setback.

A PERSON WITH A HIGH LEVEL OF SELF-COMPASSION HAS three distinct characteristics. First, he is kind and not critical of himself. Second, he recognizes the fact that he is a human being, and human beings make mistakes from time to time. Third, he takes a balanced approach toward his negative emotions whenever he fails. He takes the time to feel bad about the mistakes but does not let the negative emotions take over his spirit.

A COLLEGE PROFESSOR CARRIED OUT A STUDY TO ASSES these three elements of self-compassion. He found that among other things, people with self-compassion have an innate desire and motivation to improve themselves and are more likely to develop strong feelings of authenticity about themselves. (Authenticity, in this case, referred to the sense of being true to yourself). Motivation and authenticity are both critical in the development of a successful career.

The advantage is that both traits can be acquired, cultivated, and enhanced.

IN LIFE, ALMOST EVERYONE, INCLUDING YOURSELF, IS rooting for you to make continuous improvement. While we have already established that self-compassion is critical for this to happen, you need to do a realistic assessment of where you are and where you stand in terms of your strengths and limitations before you can move forward.

Thinking that you are better while you are not is detrimental to your growth process. For example, if you assess yourself as being able to tolerate anger and work through it by yourself while you are not, you will only succeed at repressing your emotions, which is quite destructive. A realistic, truthful assessment would require you to list truthfully where you excel and where you fail. Failure to determine the areas you ought to work on will lead you to become complacent while not acknowledging your strong points leads to defeat. Therefore, you need to take your time in quiet reflection to evaluate yourself.

WHILE GIVING YOURSELF THE LIBERTY TO MAKE MISTAKES, give others some allowance, too. The people around you are also prone to errors, both intentionally and unintentionally. You will not always have the right package delivered. You will not always have clothes that you purchased online to fit you. You will not always find that steaming cup of coffee on your desk every day. People are bound to make mistakes.

EVEN THE BEST MOVIES HAVE BLOOPERS, MULTIPLES OF them even. Sometimes, the cast of a film has to repeat something several times until they get it. If you see many of them online, the entire cast keeps laughing even if they have to repeat the same scene countless times. If movies, which are scripted and directed, have bloopers, how much more the unpredictable life we lead. Give yourself some breathing space and give the same to others. Give room for mistakes, and you will be less angry when the people around you make mistakes. You might even laugh about it.

IN THE SAME BREATH, TAKE TIME TO ENJOY THE PLEASURES that life has to offer. It is easy to get caught up in the demands of your career, your job, your family, or your perfect schedule that you forget to see the beauty that life has to offer. You may still be engrossed in something that someone did wrong two weeks ago, or you could be worried about something that will come about until you forget to be present at the moment. When you do this, you miss the little pleasures of life which are the basis of having a fun life. Celebrate the blessings that are in your life now.

YOU DO NOT HAVE TO ARRIVE EARLY AT YOUR WORKPLACE every day; be late one day. See the adrenaline rush you get before you get there. See how you dodge your boss to avoid him spotting you getting in late. Once you are late for one day, you become more thankful for the days that you arrived early.

LOOKING BACK TO YOUR EARLY MEMORIES, YOU ARE LIKELY to see that the most memorable ones, both bad and good, are those when something out of the norm happened. The day you had the most fun could be the day you defied the rules your parents set and went to the mall, not when you ate supper at 6 PM and was in bed by 8 PM. So, live a little. Go on and create those memories. Be accommodating of other people's bloopers, they will offer a great lesson for the future, and some laughs, too.

SEEK SOLUTIONS TO YOUR ISSUES

THE BENEFITS OF LEARNING HOW TO CONTROL YOUR ANGER are countless. For example, when you learn how to communicate appropriately and how to resolve conflict in a healthy way, your work life will benefit greatly. You will be able to create rapport and friendships with other people and managing your anger properly will cause you to feel healthier. It is also likely that you will sleep better in the night, your health will be on a better trend, and you could end up living longer. Here's how you leap the benefits discussed:

The first thing you need to learn how to do is to pay attention. Before you can begin to shift the reaction you give to anger, you need to spend some considerable time observing how you react when angry. Identify your anger triggers and these could range from traffic to financial issues. Next, pay attention to the signs of anger like frantic breathing or sweaty palms. Pay attention to the thoughts that come up, too. See where your thoughts go whenever you are angry or disappointed. Before you can begin to address issues related to your anger, you need to examine all there is to do with it and come up with ways to challenge every aspect of it.

Secondly, you need to seek resources available. The resources you would need to resolve anger issues could be in the form of classes, books, professional help, and others. A number of them most likely surround you. Go ahead and pay for counseling sessions or an anger management class. Many workplaces, however, offer the two services at no cost. There are also both physical and virtual support groups for which you would make an ideal candidate. If you are unsure about where to find these resources, talk to your doctor, your HR manager, or to colleagues who may have a clue about it.

Third, be focused on the solution. You will find that many strategies are focused on helping you overcome your anger and helping others around you to do the same. Majority of them we have discussed in the topics above such as mindfulness, exercise, pausing before you respond, and other relaxation techniques that are designed to help you be mindful of the responses you give to an anger trigger. Incorporate these techniques into your day, and you will find that utilizing them out in the middle of a crisis becomes quite natural.

If you feel that you cannot come up with a solution to the issues you are experiencing, it is advisable that you seek help. Many people find it difficult to coach themselves and would benefit from training by a professional or directly from a person who has dealt with similar issues in the past and overcome. Asking for help does not indicate weaknesses. It only shows your strong commitment and resolves to cause change and the ability to steer your life in the preferred direction.

Anger Management Class

The meaning of anger management is not as big as the word itself. Anger management is simply the process of learning how to recognize signs that you are angry, and then taking action to control the anger by calming down and dealing with the situation productively. Anger management is not designed to help you repress your anger; you only learn how to manage your anger alone and how to help others or deal with them when they are angry.

Some of the issues for which you may require help handling include:

- Constantly feeling irritated, hostile, and impatient
- Feeling like you need to hold on to your anger for longer every time
- Persistently focusing on negative experiences and persistently thinking negative thoughts
- Frequently arguing with others and having these fights escalate every time
- Becoming physically violent
- Giving threats of violence
- Keeping off different environments fearing that you will have anger outbursts
- Portraying out-of-control behavior like reckless driving, breaking items when angry, or doing things that put your children at risk

Anger management class will help you determine the presence of, or the absence, of the above frustrations and more so that you are better placed to express your needs, and you can stay in control of your faculties.

Anger management is done either in one-on-one sessions or in groups. A certified anger management counselor or an accredited therapist moderates the discussions, and the class can last anywhere between a few weeks and a few months.

When looking for an anger management class, make sure to verify the credentials of the therapist or the counselor. Also, ensure that the group is committed to maintaining the confidentiality of personal details expressed if you have that as a concern. Privacy and trust are also important because they create a sense of 'we' in the group, creating the impression that all members are united to fight for the same course, and that a problem to one person becomes a problem to many others.

Above all else, the anger management class needs to be one that allows you to view your anger issues from a positive angle. Some people take this class from a negative stance. They see it as a form of punishment, especially when the doctor or the boss recommends it. However, the attendee needs to reframe his thinking and understanding so that he begins to view the class as a grand opportunity to work on the self and to improve relationships.

Anger Management Support Group

An anger management support group is a therapy group made up of people who have dealt with or are in the process of dealing with anger issues. In these groups, members discuss all there is to anger, from triggers, to how they were able to deal with their problems. Members also teach other essential tools and hacks for dealing with violence. This group not only helps you overcome the issues you have now but also grows through your implementation of the solutions you have come up with. They teach you how to rebuild relationships also. A support group creates a sense of family because they celebrate with you for the progress you make and encourage you when you fail or encounter challenges.

The result of seeking solutions for your issues is that you will have a better grip of your anger. You will get the joy of having more control over your life, and more ready to overcome the challenges that life offers you. You will also begin to be more assertive in your self-expression because you do not have to be careful in your speech anymore, afraid that you may hurt someone.

In the end, learning how to manage your anger will offer you a bunch of benefits. It makes you better at communicating your needs. Anger management prevents social and psychological issues linked to anger. It keeps you from using your frustrations to get people to do what you want and turns you to a better communicator. It helps you avoid harmful and addictive coping behaviors, and enables you to maintain good health.

II

LIGHTEN UP WITH HUMOR

INSTEAD OF STRESSING AND MUSING, HOW ABOUT TURNING that anger into comedy? You see, many people fail to realize that anger is the force that drives comedy. Comedians realize this, and they will use the things that anger the society to come up with jokes. Anger does not only help to produce the things that many people can relate to but converting a problem into something people can laugh about turns the situation around. They begin to view themselves as winners, as though they are in charge of the situation, rather than as victims.

Humor heals and empowers. When you laugh about something, you assume power over it. Can you recall a time when you laughed at something that ought to have made you angry? You were probably complaining about something your spouse, parent, in-law, colleague, or friend did. When you think about it and suddenly it has you laughing, you begin to relax, and the issues start to release the hold they had on you. Some of the funniest stories we tell are those that petrified us when they happened, and now that time has passed, we have gained a better perspective and can see the humorous side of what happened.

The problem is that waiting for time to show you the humor is too long. You don't want to have suffered years of anger and become a bitter, angry person, just when the humor is beginning to reveal itself. The million-dollar question now is: how do you get to speed up this process? Here are some tips:

1. Be distracted

Researchers conducted a study where they initiated two traffic jams. In one of them, the drivers were left to their own devices, huffing, puffing, cursing, and fussing the entire time. In the other, the researchers created three distractions in the form of a puppy being walked down the road alongside the vehicles, an attractive man and a beautiful woman walking by, and a person doing stupid funny things nearby. The variables being tested in these scenarios were fuzzy and warm, sexy, and funny, respectively.

The researchers studied both groups to determine the frequency of them displaying their anger by yelling, honking, shooting their fingers, and stomping around outside their vehicles. The distracted group had fewer displays of anger, and the distraction that worked best was that of humor. From these findings, you can already see how having funny distractions, especially in situations and places that trigger your anger the most could work to keep off the anger.

• Befriend Google

The next time your anger has accumulated and you feel like your head is about to blow up with rage, especially driven by an issue you are sure should not get you mad, look on to the internet for help. Go ahead and Google funny videos and stories that have some familiarity with the issue you are handling. Find hilarious videos of people doing what you are doing or an even sillier response and laugh your heart out. The benefit of doing this is that it enables you to take your situation lightly. It also takes you out of the situation somewhat, making it easier for you to laugh at the other people's situations, and in the process, not fuss about your own.

- **Use the math**

If you spend an hour of your day laughing with friends, watching funny videos or a movie, it means that you have lessened the time you got to be angry by an hour. Therefore, if you are awake for 16 hours a day, you can only fuss for 15 of them. The more time you spend being happy, not necessarily watching movies and videos, the lesser time you have to be sad.

- **Be angry in a funny way**

Rather than expressing your anger in your usual disgruntled manner, try showing it in a way that gets you and others around you to laugh. For example, you could curse in a foreign language that others do not understand. As you circumvent your usual reactions and replies to anger, your brain will start to grasp the comic effect quicker and to let go of the negative emotions.

- **Make jokes about it**

We always assume that comedians do not get angry because they are continually making jokes and always seem happy. However, they go through the confusion, embarrassment, annoyance, and frustration that the rest of us have to endure. Without it, they would have nothing to write a comedy about. Therefore, the next time you are upset about something, especially about the not-so-heavy stuff, behave like a comedian and make fun out of it.

If by chance you are around an angry person who can't seem to crack a smile, assuming the issue he is angry about is light and the two of you are familiar with each other, go ahead and make him laugh. A story is told about a police officer who got a call to a home by neighbors who complained about the shouting match going on inside the house. As the police officer approached the front porch, the shouting escalates, and right in front of her, a TV gets thrown down from the second floor, and it instantly crashes at her feet. Instead of becoming angry and perceiving this to be a personal attack, the police officer proceeds to the front door and knocks on it. "Who's there?" A man from inside yells.

"T.V. repair," the officer yells back. The man inside laughed so hard and the laughter diffused the tension a bit, allowing the people inside to open the door and for the police officer to enter the house safely.

In tense situations, a joke is an ideal icebreaker. It lightens the mood and puts the feelings of those in the house back to perspective. In situations where you find yourself angry and cannot tell why, try to crack some jokes about it. Do not be sarcastic though, because this is not your typical environment that supports humor. Sarcasm may hurt other people's feelings.

12

FORGIVE AND LET GO

We all have been hurt at a point in life. Your child refused to heed to your counsel and started abusing drugs. Your partner cheated on you and had an affair. A colleague sabotaged your work, so he could get the promotion. A parent constantly abused you verbally, physically, and even sexually in your childhood. People have had very traumatic experiences. Wounds caused by issues like these can last a long time; they could cause you so much bitterness, anger, and a desire to retaliate.

Nevertheless, the secret to overcoming the hurt is in forgiveness. Hard as it may sound, if you do not forgive, you may end up being the one who has to pay dearly. However, when you choose to forgive, you also choose hope, happiness, peace, joy, and gratitude.

Forgiveness may have different meanings to different people, but it primarily refers to the decision to let go of the thoughts of retaliation and all manner of resentment. You may always remember the words or the act that caused you considerable pain, but forgiving lessens the grip the hurt has on you, allowing you to be free from the control of what harmed you. It is also likely that just by choosing to forgive; you will become empathetic, understanding, and even develop compassion for the person that hurt you.

FORGIVENESS DOES NOT MEAN THAT YOU EXCUSE WHAT WAS done to you either or that you become friends with the perpetrator. It is only meant to bring you some pristine peace to help you maneuver through life more easily.

SOME OF THE BENEFITS OF FORGIVING INCLUDES:

- It improves your mental health and wellness
- Boosts your self-esteem
- Enables you to have healthier relationships
- Makes you feel less depressed
- Lets you to release all the stress, anxiety, and hostility you may be holding
- Lowers your blood pressure

HOLDING A GRUDGE IS SO MUCH EASIER THAN FORGIVING. A grudge means that you are acknowledging and holding on to what a person that you loved or who should have loved you, did to you. It causes all the right emotions, those that go with what was done to you. You could feel confused, sad, and angry. However, negativity does not produce any good outcome. Therefore, if you allow these negative feelings to crowd the positive ones, you will find yourself immersed and covered up in bitterness and a strong sense of injustice.

The effects of holding a grudge include:

- A grudge causes you to lose the enriching and valued connectedness you share with others.
- It causes you to carry with you all the bitterness and anger that you hold into every relationship in your life, putting you at odds with the people in your life and denying you the opportunity to enjoy new relationships.
- Grudges cause their holders to become so engrossed in what happened in the past so much that they forget what happened in the past.
- You develop anxiety and depression.
- You may sometimes feel like despairing because you think that your life has lost meaning or that you are at odds with your belief system.

REACHING THE STATE OF FORGIVENESS

Reaching the state of forgiving is quite a difficult but achievable task. When you forgive, it means that you are living. You must also have identified the areas of your life that require now entering into a new commitment with yourself to change by becoming accepting of the value that forgiveness has to offer you and the dynamics by which it can change your healing and have a list of the people you need to forgive. If you are open to it, consider seeing a counselor or getting into a support group to receive assistance going through the situation.

ACHIEVING FORGIVENESS ALSO MAKES IT NECESSARY FOR you to acknowledge the emotions that you feel in regard to the ill that was done to you and how these emotions have affected your behavior. You must then have the purpose to release them, along with the accompanying behavior, and agree with yourself that it is time to forgive the offender. Once you have made up your mind, you are likely to go through the process more comfortably, and you will not think of turning around. Lastly, choose to walk away from a victim's identity and to release the hold the offender has had over your life.

YOU WILL NO LONGER ALLOW GRUDGES TO DEFINE YOU, and you will no longer evaluate the quality of your life by the extent to which you have been hurt.

WHEN FORGIVING IS DIFFICULT

Forgiving can be quite difficult, especially when the person who offended you does not acknowledge his responsibility, or if he or she continues to hurt you in the same way occasionally. When this happens, you are likely to feel stuck. However, you should not let anything stand in the way of your personal growth. If you already decided to forgive, nothing should keep you from doing just that, not even the offender.

THEREFORE, WHEN THIS HAPPENS, YOU CAN CHOOSE TO take up some strategies to make coping with the situation easier. First, become empathetic so that you are able to see the situation from the other party's viewpoint. Ask yourself what could be causing the person to behave as he or she does. It is possible that you would have reacted in the same way had you been in the circumstances and situation that the person is in. Think, also, of the times when you hurt others, and they forgave you, too. Consider returning the favor by forgiving an undeserving person.

. . .

Journaling, prayer, and guided meditation could also help to ease the intensity of the negative emotions. You could also talk to someone you look up to for advice on the steps you ought to take. This persOn could be an impartial loved one, a religious leader, a friend, or a mental health services provider. These people will provide you with an objective review of the situation and will help make the process of forgiving easier.

You need to be aware of the nature of forgiveness as a process that needs to be done repeatedly. You do not just wake up, forgive, and move on. Even the small mistakes need to be forgiven repeatedly so that the hurt does not build up and cause large emotional wounds.

Kindly note that you do not forgive so that the individual can change his behavior. Forgiveness is somewhat selfish because you forgive for your benefit, not for the benefit of the other party.

You should also know that forgiving does not necessitate reconciliation. Only reconcile with people with whom you share an important relationship, and even then, it is not a requirement. It would be impossible to reconcile with someone who has died or one who is unwilling to speak to you. However, this does not mean that you shouldn't forgive them. You must forgive, even when reconciliation is absent.

LET GO

Once you have forgiven, you need to let the anger and the resentment go. You must also release from your remembrance the painful words or acts and the memories of the pain, the sleepless nights, the worry, and the tears you shed. By letting go, you are releasing the emotions that are tied to each of these events.

ONCE YOU DO THAT, REMEMBERING EITHER OF THESE ACTS should not drive you to tears and the memory of the offender should not drive you to anger either. You will have released all the emotion and your brain, too, will start to bury these events so that they are no longer in your conscious part, and you are able to move on from that.

CONCLUSION

Thank you for making it through to the end of *Anger Management: 12 Step Guide to Recognize and Control Anger, Develop Emotional Intelligence, and Self Discipline*. Let's hope it was informative and able to provide you with all of the tools you need to achieve your goals whatever it is that they may be.

Each of us struggles with some unresolved emotions of anger at various points of our lives, and it is important that we learn how to recognize and deal with the negative emotions in an easy sequential way that will guarantee you emotional growth, happiness, peace, and increased satisfaction.

The next step is to take up these 12 steps to get over anger in your own life by systematically going through the process of recognizing it, understanding it, learning how to express it calmly, redirecting your attention from it, and using the strong negative emotions to drive creativity.

You now see the value of empathy and understand how it drives you to understand your offender because you get to see from the offender's unique viewpoint. You are able to realize and acknowledge the possibly unique factors that could have led the person to do what he did. Understanding makes it easier to come to terms with reality. It is possible that you could be holding on to anger caused by a person who did not even realize that they were hurting you. Others will hurt you and not care about it, nevertheless.

You have also learned how to redirect and channel your negative energy and use it as a drive for activities that demand creativity. You could try out a new hobby like drawing or painting. Some people even turn it to humor. I bet you did not know that jokes are created from the negative experiences comedian has gone through. You can also behave like a comedian and try to come up with some light jokes to help diffuse the sadness and tension that an unfortunate event causes.

You have also learned about the role of forgiveness in the management of anger. It enables you to give up the ownership and right to all negative emotions so that you are disassociated from all negative emotions. This way, even if you remember the offenders and their actions, you will be okay, neither sad nor angry.

Finally, if you found this book useful in any way, a review on Amazon is always appreciated!

DESCRIPTION

Anger Management: 12 Step Guide to Recognize and Control Anger, Develop Emotional Intelligence, and Self Discipline gives you an outline of the 12 most critical steps that you should take to manage your anger.

To that end, this book is arranged into 12 brief chapters that detail the steps you ought to take in the process of managing anger by recognizing and controlling anger to develop self-discipline and emotional intelligence that you need to maneuver through life and to guide the relationships you form with others. This book begins by indicating to you the need for you to accept your anger rather than suppressing it. It would actually be impossible for you to deal with something that you have not taken ownership of.

Once you accept that you are angry, you need to understand where the nature of your anger by determining its origins, its triggers, and the signs your body produces to indicate that the anger is about to surface. Once you realize this, you can quickly take control of the situation. The techniques the book offers to deal with your anger once you have understood it includes pausing before you react, calmly expressing your anger, practicing empathy, redirecting your focus from the triggers of anger, and how to channel your anger in a creative way.

Lastly, inside this book, you will find a discussion on how different strategies you can take to incorporate all these steps into your daily routine. For example, you will see a guide to help you in the process of forgiving and for taking up humor to overcome anger in your life. Therefore, to get started on the process of overcoming anger, get started by purchasing this book today!

Inside you will find:

- A 12-step illustration of the most critical steps to take in your quest to overcome anger
- The most explicit definition and illustration of anger and its influence in your life
- Some interesting, relatable stories to help you identify with the steps discussed in this book
- A clear depiction of the exercises that are ideal for getting rid of anger and its influences
- The most engaging discussion indicating how you ought to redirect your focus from things that anger you
- A description of empathy and the right way to express it
- Advice on how to give yourself and others a break from responsibility

Milton Keynes UK
Ingram Content Group UK Ltd.
UKHW052241120724
445583UK00046B/323